THE UNIVERSE

THE MILKY WAY

ABDO
Publishing Company

A Buddy Book **by** Fran Howard

VISIT US AT
www.abdopublishing.com

Published by ABDO Publishing Company, 8000 West 78th Street, Edina, Minnesota 55439.

Printed in the United States.

Editor: Sarah Tieck
Contributing Editor: Michael P. Goecke
Graphic Design: Maria Hosley
Cover Image: Lushpix
Interior Images: ESA (page 25); Getty Images (page 27); Lushpix (page 5, 7, 9, 29); NASA and ESA (page 23); NASA and The Hubble Heritage Team/STScI (page 17); NASA: Goddard Space Flight Center (page 28), Jet Propulsion Laboratory (page 11, 12, 29), Marshall Space Flight Center (page 19, 28); Stocktrek Images (page 15)

Library of Congress Cataloging-in-Publication Data

Howard, Fran, 1953-
  The Milky Way / Fran Howard.
      p. cm. — (The universe)
  Includes index.
  ISBN 978-1-59928-928-1
  1. Milky Way—Juvenile literature. I. Title.

QB857.7.H69 2008
523.1'13—dc22
                          2007027791

Table Of Contents

What Is The Milky Way?

At night, tiny lights dot the sky. These are stars.

In space, groups of stars form **galaxies**. A small galaxy has about 10 million stars. A large galaxy may have up to 1 trillion stars!

Our galaxy is called the Milky Way. It is a large galaxy. No one knows how many other galaxies exist. But, scientists say there could be billions!

In a very dark sky, it is possible to see the Milky Way. It looks like a thick band of stars. Most of the stars that can be seen from Earth are in the Milky Way.

Our Solar System

Scientists say **galaxies** are filled with solar systems. A solar system is a single star with many space objects, such as planets, orbiting it.

Our sun is at the center of our solar system. It is just one of many stars in the Milky Way.

Earth is one of eight planets that orbit our sun. The other planets are Mercury, Venus, Mars, Jupiter, Saturn, Uranus, and Neptune.

Dwarf planets also orbit the sun. These include Pluto, Ceres, and Eris. Comets, asteroids, and meteoroids orbit our sun, too. Also, scientists have discovered more than 100 moons in our solar system.

The sun is the only star in our solar system. But, it is one of billions of stars in our galaxy! Some scientists think our galaxy could have as many as 400 billion stars.

A Closer Look

Galaxies contain dust, gas, stars, and other space objects. Scientists think that there is a very large black hole at the center of the Milky Way.

A black hole is not really a hole. It is an area of space with very strong gravity. The pull of gravity in a black hole is so strong that even light is trapped!

The black hole at the Milky Way's center is huge. Scientists say it is about 3 million times larger than our sun!

Different Shapes

Scientists group **galaxies** by shape. There are irregular, elliptical, and spiral galaxies.

Irregular galaxies are some of the smallest. They have no particular shape. Many new stars form in irregular galaxies. Yet, they have both old and young stars.

Some of the largest galaxies are elliptical. But, there are also small elliptical galaxies. Elliptical galaxies are shaped like stretched-out circles. They have many old stars.

About 30 percent of galaxies are spiral, and 10 percent are irregular. The remaining 60 percent are elliptical.

The Milky Way is a spiral-shaped **galaxy**. Spiral galaxies have many young stars.

Stars, gas, and dust gather to form a spiral-shaped galaxy's arms. These arms spiral around the galaxy's center. Scientists say the Milky Way has four to six arms.

The NGC 7331 galaxy *(above)* and the Milky Way are both spiral shaped.

Our Solar System

Center of the Milky
Way Galaxy

Our solar system is located in
one of the Milky Way's arms.

Circling The Center

Stars orbit the center of a **galaxy** like Earth orbits the sun. Old and dying stars are closer to the middle. Millions of younger stars are spread out in the galaxy's long arms.

Both old and young stars in the Milky Way are visible in our night sky.

Galaxies have orbits, too. Several galaxies can group into a cluster. The galaxies in the cluster all circle the same center of gravity.

The Milky Way is part of a binary galaxy system. This means that two galaxies orbit one center together.

Satellites have taken images of two galaxies orbiting the same center. The Milky Way and Andromeda galaxies orbit in a similar way.

Traveling Our Galaxy

In space, distance is measured in light-years and light-minutes. One light-year is how far light would travel in one year. This is very far. Light travels nearly 6 trillion miles (10 trillion km) in one year!

The Milky Way is a large **galaxy**. It is about 100,000 light-years across.

The Andromeda galaxy is the closest spiral galaxy to the Milky Way. Still, scientists say it is about 2 million light-years away.

Discovering The Milky Way

Many scientists think the Milky Way formed about 14 billion years ago! Scientists have many **theories** about how this happened. They have been discussing this topic for many years. Still, no one knows for sure how our **galaxy** formed!

The big bang theory says that the universe started out smaller than a grapefruit. Over time, and with great force, it grew. Now it includes galaxies, stars, and planets.

Scientists have studied stars for many years. And as telescopes became more powerful, they also started studying the Milky Way.

Many important discoveries have been made over the years. In the late 1700s, British astronomer William Herschel began mapping the Milky Way's stars. In 2005, astronomers proved the Milky Way was a barred spiral **galaxy**.

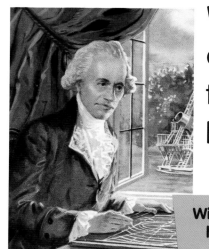

William Herschel drew his maps by hand.

Barred galaxies have a central bar-shaped area filled with stars. Astronomers think stars form there.

Exploring The Milky Way

Scientists are still using powerful telescopes to learn about the Milky Way. Some of the telescopes are on Earth. Others are in space.

Space-based telescopes lie outside Earth's **atmosphere**. This allows them to capture more detailed images of distant space objects.

One space-based telescope is the *Rossi X-ray Timing Explorer*. It has orbited Earth since 1995 and mapped the Milky Way. Scientists are studying this map. It has revealed that there are more objects in our **galaxy** than scientists had thought!

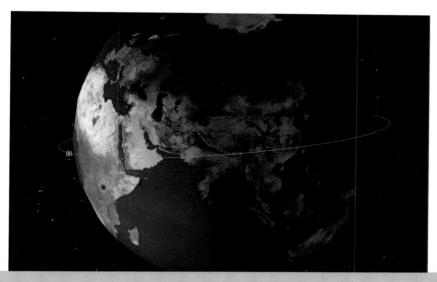

The *Hubble Space Telescope* has been orbiting Earth since 1990. It has taken some of the most detailed images of the Milky Way.

NASA launched the *Spitzer Space Telescope* in August 2003. It has provided scientists with some high-quality images of deep space. Deep space includes any region of space outside our solar system.

European scientists have been using a powerful ground-based telescope to study the Milky Way. This telescope is at the La Silla Paranal Observatory in Chile.

The La Silla Paranal Observatory helped European scientists discover a large area of star formation in the Milky Way.

Fact Trek

Andromeda is the closest **galaxy** to the Milky Way. Scientists say that these two galaxies are moving toward each other at 300,000 miles (500,000 km) per hour.

Andromeda galaxy

Galaxies can hit each other. Scientists say that Andromeda and the Milky Way could collide in 3 billion years!

Many myths surround the **origin** of the Milky Way. One Greek myth says each star in the Milky Way is a dairy cow. And, the **galaxy**'s blue glow is from their milk. Some say this is why we call it the Milky Way.

Black holes can be very large. Some are 100 million times as large as our sun!

Black holes can suck in stars!

Voyage To Tomorrow

Scientists are continuing to learn about the Milky Way. Several powerful space telescopes are orbiting Earth. These telescopes regularly send back new information about the Milky Way. Scientists study this information to learn new things about our **galaxy**.

The *Spitzer Space Telescope* trails behind Earth as it orbits the sun.

Important Words

atmosphere the layer of gases that surrounds space objects, including planets, moons, and stars.

galaxy a large group of stars and planets.

launch to send off with force.

NASA National Aeronautics and Space Administration.

origin the source or the beginning of something.

theory an explanation of how or why something happens.

Web Sites

To learn more about the **Milky Way,** visit ABDO Publishing Company on the World Wide Web. Web sites about the **Milky Way** are featured on our Book Links page. These links are routinely monitored and updated to provide the most current information available.

www.abdopublishing.com

INDEX